HE[illegible] GUIDE

Contents

The Westgate and the new Guildhall, formerly Holy Cross Church.

The City of Canterbury

Canterbury is the cultural and historic centre of Kent. Its unique character was wrought out of the need to accommodate the thousands of medieval pilgrims who flocked here to be absolved from mortal sin.

The vitality and enthusiasm of medieval Christianity created the Cathedral. The medieval town with its pilgrim hostels, markets and churches is revealed and explored in this guide.

When the town was firebombed in June 1942, the character of what had, by then, become a sleepy market town was changed overnight. Many of the medieval buildings were burned to the ground, others were demolished in the post-war reconstruction.

Today, the town has an air of renewal, with new buildings springing up throughout, sparking a lively local debate on their architectural merits, and once again the streets throng with visitors from home and abroad.

Roman Beginnings

The Roman Theatre, a reconstruction by Canterbury Archaeological Trust, drawn by John A. Bowen.

Our picture of Canterbury's earliest beginnings is becoming clearer thanks to the work of the Canterbury Archaeological Trust. There is evidence of a pre-Roman settlement within the city walls but nothing to suggest a town.

The Roman town of *Durovernum Cantiacorum* was constructed from the second century onwards. It had a huge 'D' shaped theatre, temples and a forum. The walls we see today are medieval but were built upon the remains of the Roman walls which were constructed about AD 270-90 in response to Saxon raids along the coast.

By the fall of the Empire most of the townspeople would have been Christians. But urban life collapsed during the first half of the 5th century when the town and its public buildings were abandoned and left to decay. Into the ruins stepped settlers from Denmark, the Jutes, who set up primitive camps in and around the town. By the end of the 6th century there was a thriving Kentish kingdom centred around Canterbury engaged in trade with the Merovingian Franks across the Channel.

The street plan developed during this period and despite heavy war-time bombing much has survived.

Christianity and the Kings of Kent

Reconstruction of the Reculver Cross, symbol of 7th century Kentish Christianity, drawing by Julie Beer.

It was the marriage of Bertha, a Frankish princess who was also a Christian, to Ethelbert, King of Kent, which paved the way for the mission of St Augustine to evangelize the English and found the Cathedral at Canterbury in AD 597.

Before Augustine's arrival Bertha and her priest had been permitted to practice their religion privately. Each day she and her confessor left the confines of the walled city through the Queningate and travelled to their private chapel at St Martin's Church.

After the conversion of Ethelbert and his court Augustine established his group around one of the town's crumbling Roman churches, probably on the site of the present Cathedral, and restored it with the help of the King. He also founded a monastery outside the city walls for his companions which also served as a place of Royal burial.

In the following centuries two of England's greatest Benedictine houses evolved, the first at St Augustine's Abbey, the second, Christ Church Priory at the Cathedral. From that point, until their dissolution in 1538, these religious institutions dominated city life.

In the early years the two religious communities fought over the burial rights of the Archbishops and relics of the saints. Ultimately, Christ Church won the battle for the possession of the best holy relics as it was they who owned the saintly remains of murdered Archbishop Thomas Becket. Following a series of miracles at his tomb, the shrine of St Thomas of Canterbury became one of the most important places of pilgrimage in Europe, comparable with Lourdes or Santiago de Compostella today.

Pilgrims, Monks & Friars

The importance medieval man placed on holy relics is hard to understand because his view of the world was universal, not scientific like ours. The material world was viewed as in a constant state of flux and intrinsically evil. The world of the spirit, was by contrast immutable and good. Holy relics were a tangible link with the beneficent cosmic forces of the universe which protected Kings, cured the sick and gave blessings to those who venerated them.

After Archbishop Thomas Becket was murdered in 1174 thousands flocked to his tomb seeking help and blessings from the martyr. The visitors, then as now, needed accommodation, food and souvenirs to mark their visit. Huge new pilgrim hostels were built around the Butter Market and at the Eastbridge Hospital. The Cathedral was rebuilt and thousands of badges and little bottles, *ampulla,* containing a watered down spot of the martyr's blood were sold.

In 1386 Geoffrey Chaucer started work on The Canterbury Tales. The work revolves around a band of 30 pilgrims who set off from the Tabard Inn in Southwark to visit the shrine of St Thomas. The Prologue is a concise portrait of a group of everyday medieval characters, the stories themselves are gleaned from all over Europe. The Tales are written in the French romantic style using the best English of the day. His fine tomb in Westminster Abbey describes Chaucer as "The Father of English Poetry."

When Henry VIII famously broke with Rome the practice of pilgrimage had all but disappeared. In the dissolution of the monasteries which followed after 1536 St Augustine's Abbey was closed and the Abbot's Hall converted into a royal palace for the arrival of Henry's 4th wife, Anne of Cleaves. Christ Church Priory was converted into a school, the King's School. Many of the original priory buildings are still used by the school today.

The gold plate and jewels which covered Becket's sacred tomb were removed to Henry's Exchequer and the shrine demolished. The country was briefly returned to the 'Faith' by Mary Tudor in 1553. Mary and her Archbishop, Reginald Pole, set about restoring the old heresy laws and Canterbury was thrown into one of its most grisly and turbulent periods of history. City artisans and shopkeepers, including ten women, were imprisoned and burnt at the stake for their Protestant faith in "Martyrs' Field" where a monument stands in their honour.

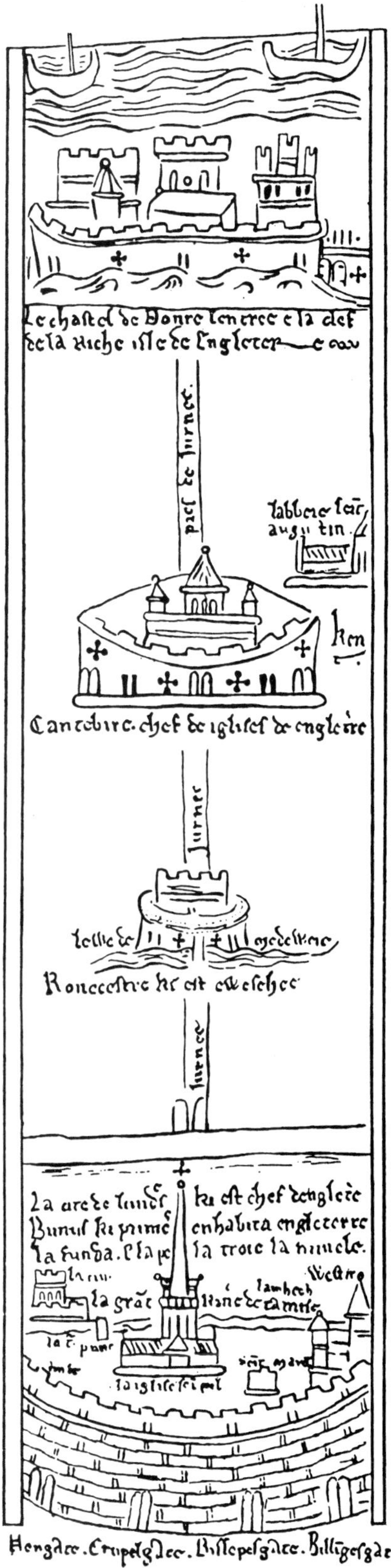

13th century 'Pilgrim Map', London to Dover.

A Sleepy Market Town

With the demise of the monasteries and the establishment of the Church of England Canterbury slipped out of national prominence. The Archbishop's seat of influence became his London Palace at Lambeth.

Religious persecutions in Europe led protestant refugees from France and Belgium to settle in the town. These Walloon settlers established the city as a centre for the silk industry in the 16th century. Likewise, English dissenters including the local Cushman family, the Allertons and the Chilterns finally fled England for greater religious freedom in the New World in 1620.

The English Revolution with its intolerance of 'Catholic' practices in the English Church gave rise to a bout of iconoclasm in the town. Stained glass windows and religious statues were smashed including the Cathedral font. Parliament's banning of the celebration of Christmas caused riots in the street. When Charles II was restored to the throne in 1660 the citizens hanged their Parliamentary Governor from the Westgate.

The army arrived in strength during the Napoleonic Wars and has stayed to the present day. The Kent Regiment or 'Buffs' has disappeared through a series of regimental re-organisations and amalgamations; the regiment stationed here today is the Princess of Wales's Royal Regiment, more popularly known as Di's Guys.

This sleepy market town with its coaching inns, clerics and weekly cattle market made slow progress with public health improvements in the 19th century, the towns people suffering foul air and poor sanitation. Although there was no great industrial development the town was one of the first in the country to benefit from a passenger railway service when a line was constructed to Whitstable, some 6 miles north, in 1830.

The biggest change to the city came on a single night in June 1942 when it was firebombed by the Luftwaffe. The Cathedral was more or less untouched but the town was devastated. The post war reconstruction is about to reach its culmination as the last of the bomb sites is swallowed up for property development.

St Peter's Street, from a 19th century guide to Canterbury.

Canterbury became part of the second wave of Red Brick, perhaps more accurately, Grey Concrete university towns in 1962. Since then the University, and more recently Christ Church College have re-created Canterbury's reputation for academic excellence and passionate intellectual debate.

Canterbury People

Site of the old Rush Market, Sun Street.

Throughout its history the city has been home to many colourful characters, intellectuals and writers. There are also five local saints after which some of the town's finest churches, buildings and streets are named.

St Augustine

In 596 Augustine, an Italian monk , was chosen to head a mission of thirty monks to evangelize the Anglo-Saxons. Although he received a cautious welcome from Ethelbert, King of Kent, he was given a house in Canterbury and allowed to preach. By 601 Ethelbert and his court had been converted to Christianity whereupon St Augustine went on to found the Cathedrals at Canterbury and Rochester and the monastery of St Peter and St Paul, later known as St Augustine's Abbey in Canterbury.

St Dunstan

Born into a noble family near Glastonbury, Dunstan (909-988) was a great church reformer and Archbishop of Canterbury. He re-established the Rule of St Benedict in monasteries across the land after the chaos caused by Viking attacks. He is more often remembered for his work as a manuscript illuminator, musician and metalworker and is traditionally shown holding the devil by the nose with a pair of blacksmith's tongs. The church bearing his dedication is at the top of St Dunstan's Street and was the family church of Margaret Roper, daughter of St Thomas More. More's decapitated head rests in the crypt.

St Alphege

Alphege, first of the Canterbury martyrs, was an English monk who became Archbishop in 1005. By 1011 the Danes led by King Canute had defeated the English King Ethelred, and had overrun much of southern England. In September of that year they besieged and captured Canterbury taking Alphege and holding him for a ransom of £3,000 at Greenwich. Alphege forbade his supporters to pay whereupon the infuriated Danes tied the old man to a post and pelted him with ox bones until he was dead. Alphege was eventually buried at Canterbury and the discovery that his remains were uncorrupted a century later led to his canonisation. The church bearing his dedication is now the Canterbury Centre.

Geoffrey Chaucer

In 1386 Geoffrey Chaucer started work on *'The Canterbury Tales'*. His inspiration for the characters came from his contact with the merry bands of pilgrims making their way to Canterbury through his role as Parliamentary representative for Kent and as a Thames Commissioner. He spent most of his working life in London and abroad as a royal diplomat. He made a fortuitous marriage to Philippa Payne Roet whose sister ultimately became the wife of the vastly influential John of Gaunt. His fortunes plummeted after her death as her royal pensions ceased and the capricious royal patronage he had enjoyed was withdrawn. His writing continued until his death, on Christmas Eve 1399, despite his financial problems. This foundation work of English Literature has never lost its appeal and has been studied by scholars and students through the ages.The Chaucer Heritage Trust organises an annual summer festival in London and the 'Canterbury Tales' Spring Pilgrimage. The Trust, which can be found at 22, St Peters Street, has an international membership of Chaucer enthusiasts.

William Somner

William Somner published Antiquities of Canterbury in 1640. This first history of the city proved an invaluable catalogue of offending art and architecture to the iconoclasts lead by Rev. Richard Culmer, otherwise known as 'Blue Dick'. Somner lived and worked in the house in Castle Street where he had been born. A staunch Royalist, he presented a copy of his remarkable book to the restored Charles II on his arrival at Dover. He also funded the installation of a new font in the Cathedral, the original having been destroyed by Blue Dick and his followers.

Archbishop Stephen Langton

Archbishop Stephen Langton, an English born European intellectual, was forced on a reluctant King John by Pope Innocent III with the full force of the French army behind him. Before taking up his position in 1207, Langton had been a professor at Paris. His work there consisted of writing highly technical biblical commentaries, otherwise known as *glosses*, from which we get the expression, *'to put a gloss on something'*. Langton was instrumental in forcing King John to sign the Magna Carta and held the Tower of London for the Barons to ensure John's submission to their demands.

Lanfranc

The installation of Lanfranc, the first Norman Archbishop, in 1070 led to a radical shake up of religious organisation and practice in England and gave Canterbury a direct link to the intellectual hot house of the Abbey at Bec in Normandy. The Danish invasions earlier in the century had taken a heavy toll on the economic and intellectual life of the country. Lanfranc injected new life into the monasteries improving their finances and buildings and brought their liturgical practices up to date. Lanfranc was the first in a procession of European intellectuals who inherited the See of Canterbury.

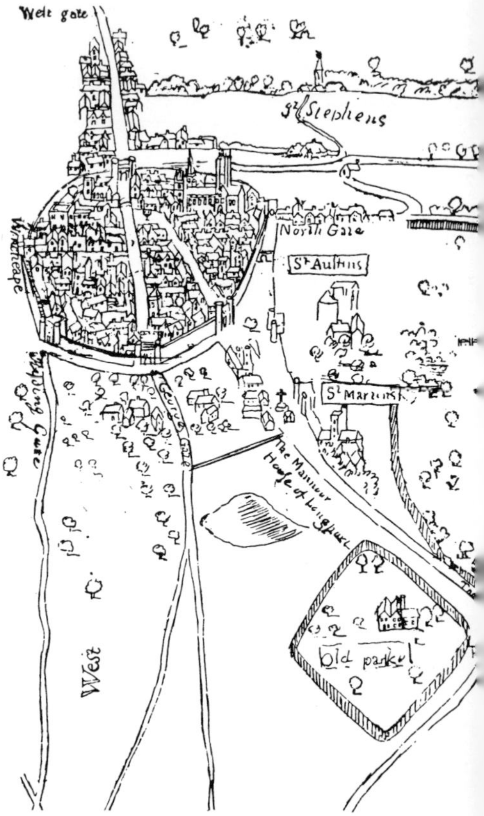

St Anselm

St Anselm, Archbishop from 1089, is acknowledged as one of the greatest medieval minds. He studied under Lanfranc at Bec then became Archbishop following the death of his mentor. He established the investiture of bishops with a staff and ring throughout Europe and the 'Primacy' of Canterbury over York. Famed throughout Europe

Christopher Marlowe

A dramatist, poet, translator and spy, Marlowe was baptised at St George's Church on February 26, 1563. He was educated at the King's School and Corpus Christi College. He died in a Deptford tavern brawl at the age of twenty-nine. In his short life he aroused, in his contemporaries, strong views on his lifestyle and work. He had grown up in Canterbury during a period of great religious intolerance which led him to atheism. His work is overshadowed by the genius of his rival Shakespeare but is considered to be the foundation stone of English tragedy. His plays Dr Faustus and Edward II have recently enjoyed a successful revival.

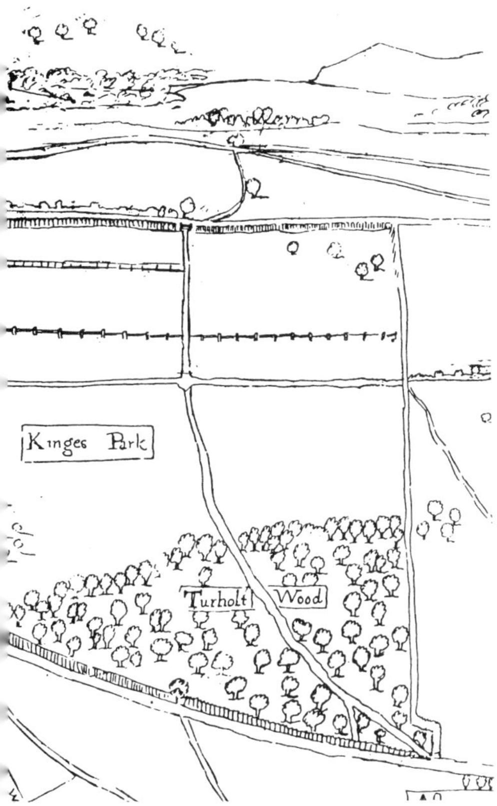

Canterbury from the east, late 17th century map.

for his theological teaching he attracted many pupils to Canterbury. His philosophical works together with his beautiful devotional writings and prayers had a profound influence on European intellectual life into the 19th century. The city's Catholic Comprehensive school is named after him.

St Thomas Becket

Thomas Becket, Canterbury's most famous Archbishop, was born in London to a wealthy family and educated at Merton Abbey and Paris. He joined the court of Archbishop Theobald of Canterbury and was sent to Bologna and Auxerre to study law. He became Archdeacon of Canterbury in 1154 where he was used by Theobald as a negotiator with the Crown. When Henry II succeeded to the throne in 1155 he chose Becket as his Chancellor.

In 1162 Henry obtained Becket's election as Archbishop of Canterbury. Adapting to his new role he opposed Henry on the issues of church taxation and the jurisdiction of secular courts over clerics. The long and bitter struggle between church and state led to exile, and eventually in 1170, to death for Becket. Within ten years of his murder there had been 703 miracles at his tomb. He was hailed as a martyr for Christ and church liberty.

Mary Tourtel

The author of the world famous Rupert Bear Stories, Mary Tourtel, was born at 51, Palace Street in 1874. Rupert Bear, dressed in his bright red sweater and yellow checked trousers, first appeared in the Daily Express in 1920. Along with his Nutwood friends Mary Tourtel's creation has remained a firm children's favourite appearing in books and cartoon animations. There is a special Rupert Bear exhibition at the Canterbury Heritage Museum.

Wat Tyler

The Peasant's Revolt of 1381 was led by a character from Dartford called Walter the Tyler against the imposition of a Poll Tax. He and his ragged band entered Canterbury on the Monday after Trinity Sunday. They terrified the monks and townsfolk when they beheaded three of the town's richest men in the street. Having extracted promises of support they marched for London gaining hundreds of supporters along the way. Entering the capital on 13th June, a drunken orgy of xenophobic killing ensued. Men from Kent stormed the Tower of London murdering the Archbishop, Simon Sudley; the Chancellor, Robert Hales; and the Treasurer; William Appuldore as revenge for their harsh extraction of this pernicious tax.

Top left: Romanesque tower on the south-east transept, known as St Anselm's.

Top right: Heraldic decoration on Christ Church Gate.

Above: Statue of Christ Blessing by Klaus Ringwald, Christ Church Gate.

Left: Lavishly carved 17th century door, Christ Church Gate.

The Cathedral

The south-west prospect of Christ Church Cathedral.

It takes about 1 hour 30 minutes to see the Precincts, Priory ruins and inside the Cathedral. Admission: Adults £2, concessions £1. Restricted opening on Sundays: 12.30 to 2.30 pm and 4.30 to 5.30 pm.

Start your visit in the Butter Market in front of Christ Church Gate.

Christ Church Gate

This gate was commissioned by Henry VII to celebrate the ill fated marriage of his son, Prince Arthur, to Catherine of Aragon. The gate is built in the Gothic style and was completed in 1521, there is a modern figure of Christ by Klaus Ringwald in the centre panel. Henry, not wishing to return Catherine to Spain after Arthur's death, married her to his second son Henry, later Henry VIII. It was their famous divorce which ultimately led to the foundation of the Church of England.

Introduction

Through the gate you enter the Cathedral Precincts with its houses, shop and Information Centre, disabled visitors can pick up a leaflet here and anyone wishing to take photographs inside the Cathedral should buy a permit.

Before entering the Cathedral a walk around the Precincts and the Priory ruins is recommended. If the weather is bad or you are short of time turn to page 19.

There are three complexes of buildings within the precincts: the Cathedral, the ruins and buildings of Christ Church Priory and the Archbishop's Palace (not open to the public). Canterbury Cathedral, unlike its continental counterparts, was built by its Priors not its Archbishops. Excavations in 1993 exposed the foundations of the Saxon cathedral (c. 800-1070) which would have been one of the largest buildings in western Christendom. The present building is deemed to be one of the most beautiful buildings in the world and is designated a World Heritage Site.

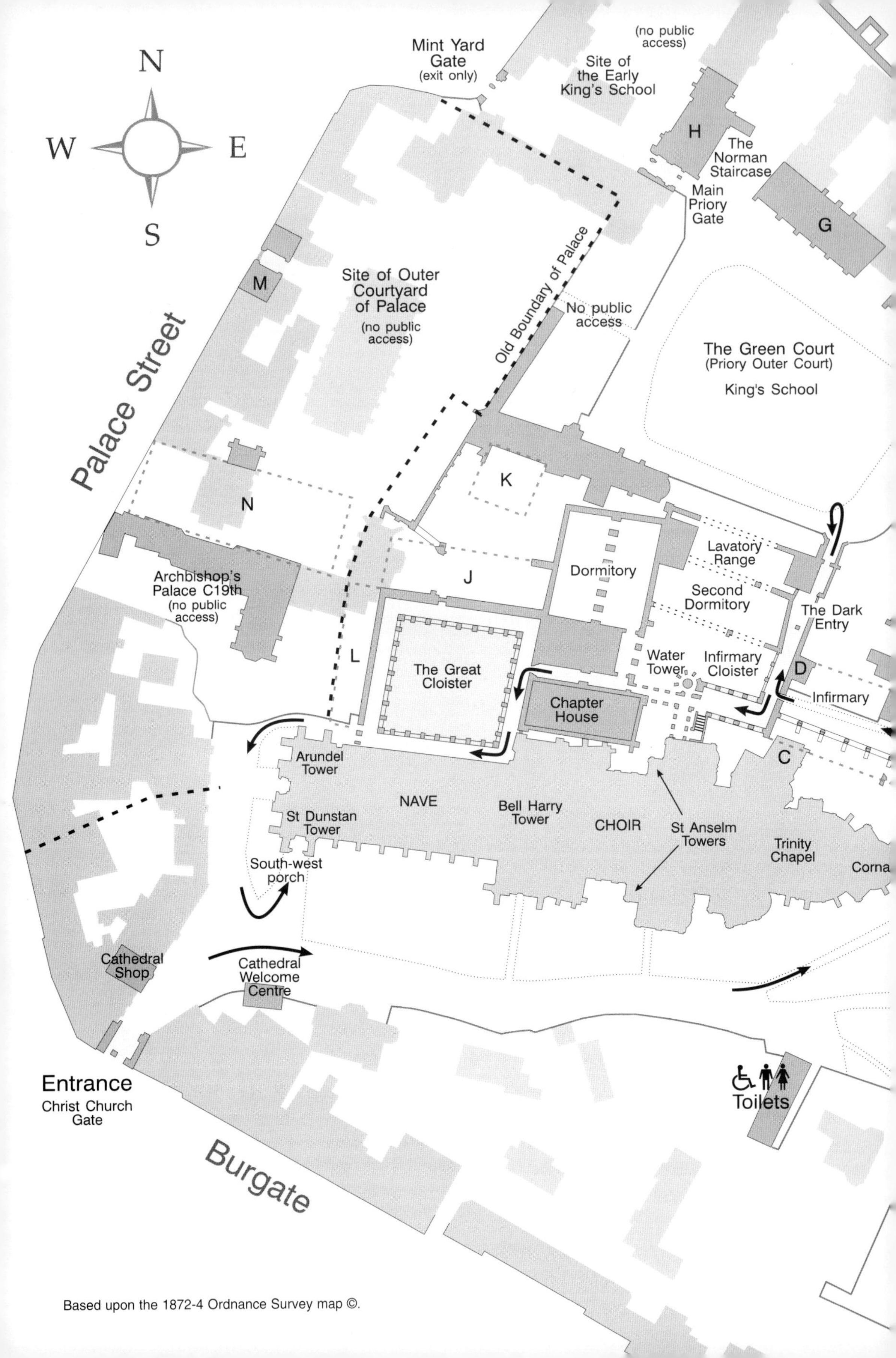

Based upon the 1872-4 Ordnance Survey map ©.

The Precincts and Priory

Many of the buildings in the Precincts have their roots in the Priory or the Archbishop's Palace (none of these have public access).

A C14th Guest Hall.
B Infirmarer's Dining Hall.
C C12th Treasury.
D Checker Tower, stairs to counting house.
E 12th Bathhouse, then Prior's Guest House, now the Deanery.
F Bakery and Granary.
G Brewery.
H Remains of C12th Guest Hall.
J Site of Dining Hall.
K Site of Kitchen
L Cellarer's and Novices' Lodging.
M Archbishop's Palace Gate.
N Remains of Archbishop's Great Hall.

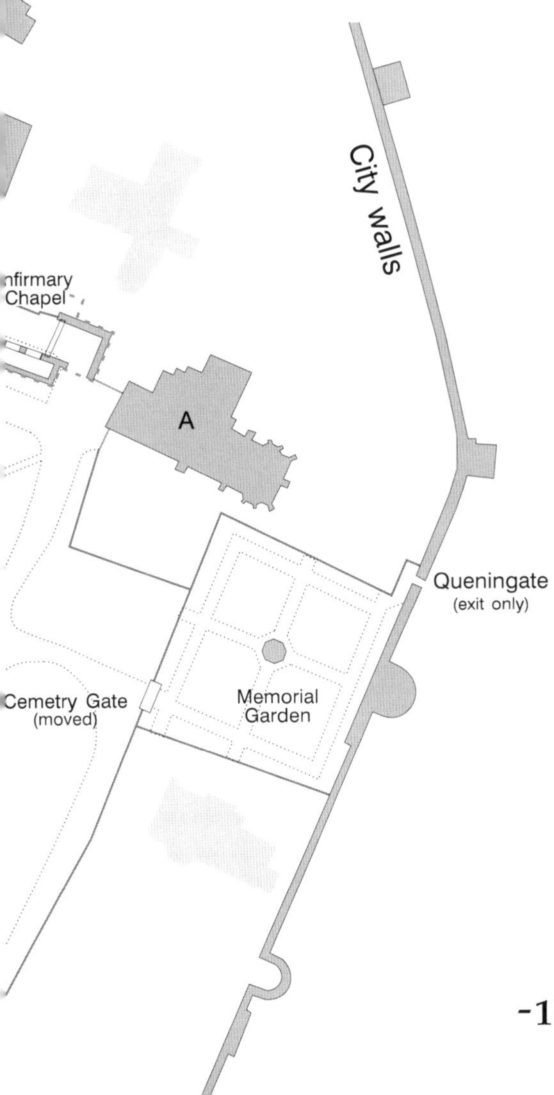

This guided walk around the Precincts and Priory Ruins takes about 30 minutes

Looking at the cathedral from Christ Church gate you see the fine **south-west porch.** The two towers at the west end are the **Arundel Tower** and **St Dunstan Tower** which today houses the Cathedral's bells. The central tower, standing some 300 feet high, is the **Bell Harry Tower**, completed around 1500. The original work by Henry Yevele was extended and enhanced by John Wastell, architect of King's College Chapel, Cambridge.

Further east you will see the beautiful **St Anselm Tower**. Highly decorated with Romanesque motifs, its roof and interlaced arcades are particularly fine.

Walking along the south side you can see many architectural styles. The changes can be most easily identified by the different shapes of the windows and arches. The pointed arches of the nave are Gothic, dating to the late 14th century; the rounded arches of the choir, known as Romanesque or Norman, date from the 12th century. The upper part of the choir and the Trinity Chapel with its mix of rounded and pointed arches marks the introduction of the Gothic style to England.

The circular structure at the end which looks like an addition is contemporary with the Trinity Chapel. This, the circular **Corona chapel,** was designed to hold one of the holy relics of St Thomas.

Pass around the Corona chapel. You are now entering the complex of buildings that was once Christ Church Priory, one of the richest Benedictine monasteries in England. Ahead you see the ruins of the Monk's Infirmary and to the right, the Infirmary Chapel built in the Norman style.

Walk through the ruins and enter the **Infirmary cloister.** The grassy space beyond the arcade was the Infirmary garden where medicinal herbs were grown. Turn right

The Norman staircase.

The King's School

The school dates to around the 13th century when it was known as the Archbishop's or Almonry School. It was recognised by Henry VIII as part of the Cathedral's foundation in 1541 and required the Dean and Chapter to provide education for 50 poor scholars. The school was reformed in the 19th century becoming one of England's most prestigious Public Schools. Christopher Marlowe was one its earliest pupils, since then many illustrious characters have passed through its portals; Hugh Walpole, W. Somerset Maugham and Monty, Viscount Montgomery of El Alamein to name only a few.

through **The Dark Entry**, reputed to be haunted by the ghost of Nell Cook, an encounter with her ghost is said to bring death within the year!

Beyond The Dark Entry you will see the **Green Court**, a lawn surrounded by a series of buildings with peg tile roofs. These are now part of the King's School but were originally the domestic buildings of the monastery. The court served as a functional yard which would have been filled with people going about their daily tasks.

Diagonally to the left is a fabulous yellow stone building known as the **Norman Staircase**. This series of covered steps led to the Norman Aula Nova which was the medieval equivalent of hotel accommodation for important pilgrims, today it serves as part of the King's School.

Return through the Dark Entry, following the Infirmary Cloister around to the right then enter its grassed courtyard.

Across to the left are the ruins of the monk's **dormitory** and behind you, built into the side of the cloister is a little **water tower**. This tower was built as part of an extensive water and sanitation system which was inspired and executed during Prior Wibert's ad-

Above: Monk's Infirmary Ruins and Checker Tower.

Below: Dormitory ruins with the King's School beyond.

Right: The Trinity Chapel.

ministration in the 12th century. Fresh water was supplied from springs to the north of the city where it ran through a series of settling tanks to clean it, before being piped to the monastery.

Turn back into the cloister and continue through the passage to **The Great Cloister.**

The Great Cloister is late 14th century Gothic with elaborate fan vaulting for the ceiling. The bosses show the coats of arms of the families who contributed to its construction. It may be the fourth cloister to have stood on this site. The cloisters were used by the monks as a place of work and recreation.

To the left is the **Chapter House** (not always open to the public). This was the monk's meeting room. The election of the Priors and Archbishops as well as the discussion of building plans, finance, and religious issues took place here. Notice the magnificent 15th century roof and the massive Victorian stained glass window.

Leave the Cloister at the opposite corner and make your way round the west end. To the right you will see the gated entrance to the **Archbishop's Palace** (not open to the public). The Palace was renovated at the turn of the century by Archbishop Temple making it possible for the Archbishops to reside within the city for the first time in nearly 300 years.

Go past the Great West Door to the South West Porch to begin your tour of the interior of the Cathedral.

Inside th

This guided tour of the Cathedral takes about 45 minutes. Enter the Cathedral by the south west porch below the St Dunstan Tower.

The Nave

The main body of the church, the Nave, was rebuilt in 1377 by architect Henry Yevele, designer of Westminster Hall. It took 28 years to complete. It is built in the Perpendicular Gothic style and throughout the medieval period this was the public part of the Cathedral. It replaced what must have been an equally magnificent nave in the Romanesque style, which had galleries and a second floor running the length of both aisles.

Before you make your way down the Nave turn to look at the **West Window (1).** Set in the lower panels of the window are some of the oldest pieces of stained glass in Europe. Thirteen of the large figures in the bottom two rows of the window date to the begining of the 13th century. The lower central panel shows Adam digging, dressed in an animal skin, hooves still attached, having been cast out of paradise. His medieval spade is wooden with iron only on the cutting edge.

In the north aisle you will see the black and white baroque **font (2)** donated by William Somner, a faithful Royalist, the original having been smashed by Cromwell's followers. Until the 18th century the side aisles were packed with alters, shrines and chantry chapels. In medieval times these were places where prayers were offered for the souls of the dead. There are many interesting monuments lining the walls of the nave today, particularly on the north side, where there is a representation of a burial at sea in the **Hales Family monument (3).**

At the end of the north aisle go into the Martyrdom Chapel in the North West Transept.

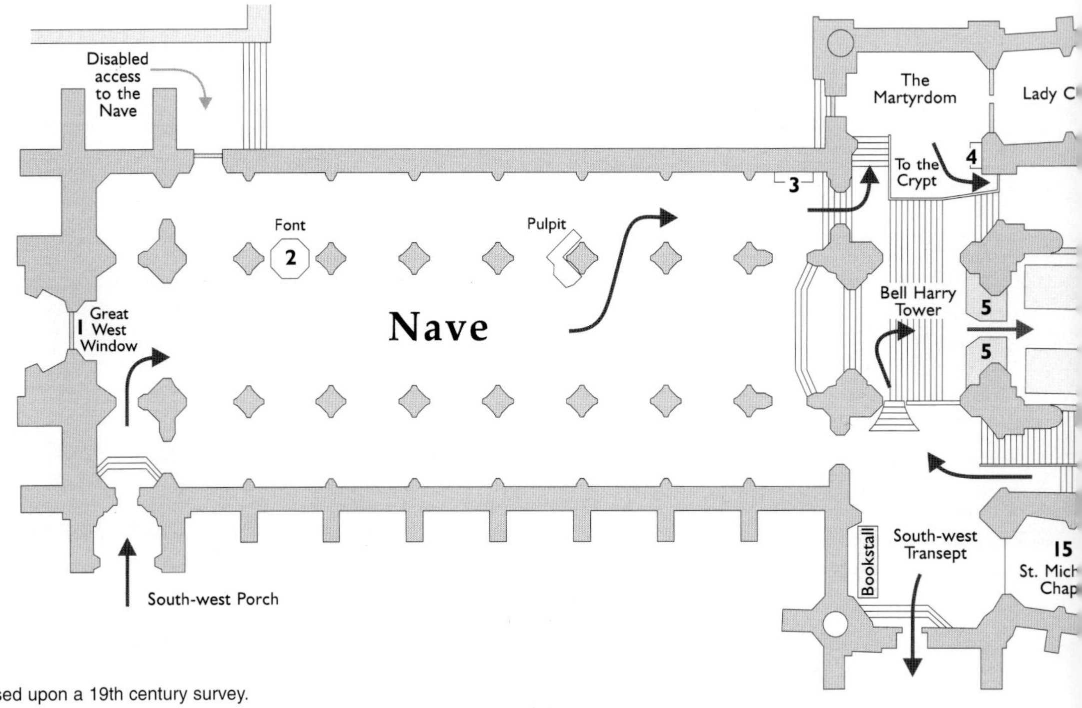

Based upon a 19th century survey.

Cathedral

The Martyrdom

Thomas Becket was murdered here on 29th December 1170, by four knights; Richard Brito, Hugh de Moreville, Reginald Fitzurse and William de Tracy.

Today the spot is marked by a new **altar (4)** with a sculpture of swords and a cross. There is also a plaque to mark the visit of Pope John Paul II in 1982. In medieval times the Altar of the Sword's Point displayed two relics, part of Brito's sword which had broken off in the attack and a ring containing a fragment of the saint's brain set under crystal.

Although the NW Transept has under gone many alterations over the centuries the floor where Becket fell has never been replaced. **Enter the Crypt by the steps to the right of the Altar of the Sword's Point.**

The Murder

Becket, friend and former Chancellor to Henry II, had been chosen as Archbishop so that Henry could control the Church, which operated independently of the state. But Becket took his new role as a religious leader seriously and refused to co-operate with Henry's plans. Henry could not believe his misfortune and moaned constantly about this troublesome turncoat.

The knights, unknown to Henry and in the belief they were doing him a great service, entered the Cathedral and called for the Archbishop who was at the late afternoon service of Vespers in the Choir. He came down the steps in the winter darkness to meet them at the door, an argument and tussle ensued, whereupon de Tracy called out to the knights to strike with their swords. He was killed by the third blow which sliced off the top of his head.

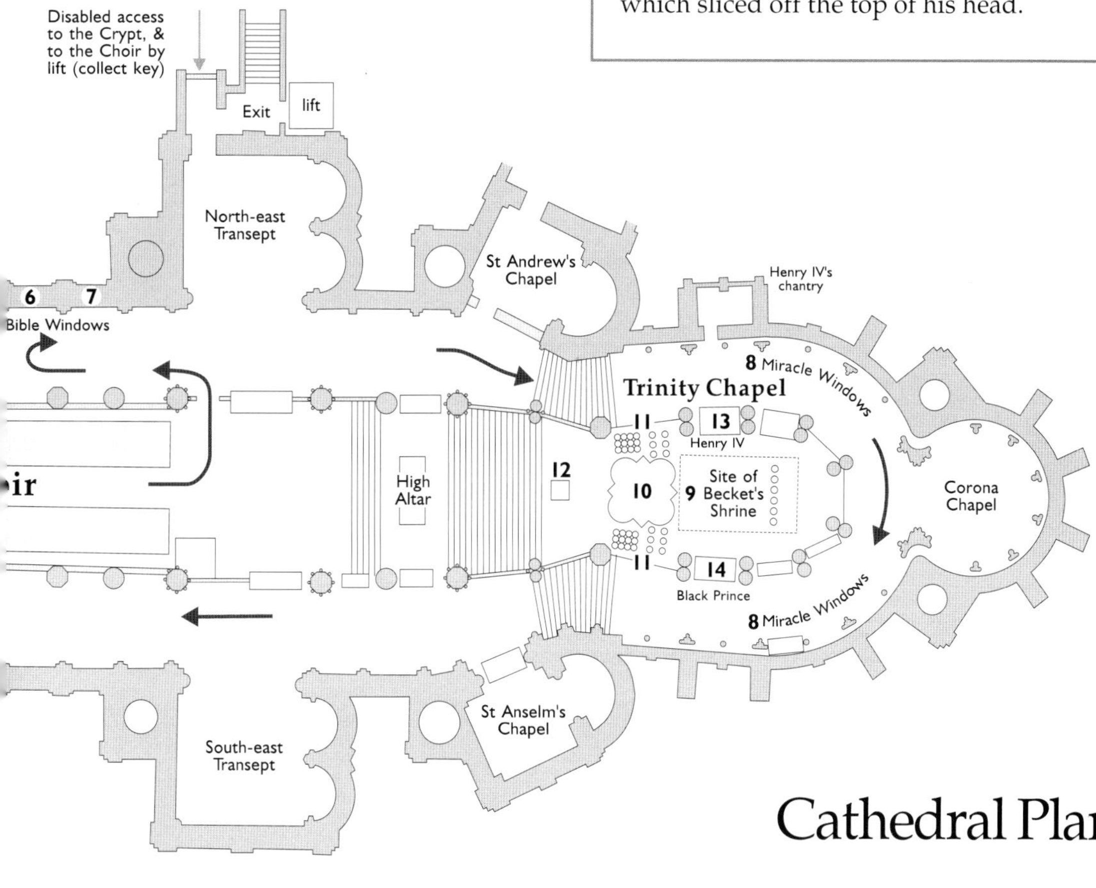

Cathedral Plan

The C13th Jesse Tree in the Corona Chapel.

The Crypt and Treasury

Enter the semi-darkness of the crypt and you are in the oldest surviving part of the medieval cathedral. On the right you can see the Cathedral Treasury, a small museum housing precious church plate and regalia (open summer season only). Look up and around and you will see the beautifully carved, short stumpy columns supporting the Cathedral above you. The exquisite Romanesque capitals (column tops) are amongst the finest examples of early medieval stone work in Europe.

In the centre, the chapel of Our Lady of the Undercroft has a 14th century screen and a beautiful painted ceiling.

At the end of the first part of the crypt you will come across two large columns set in the curve of the aisles, these were inserted after the fire in 1174 to carry the arcades above eastward to form the Trinity Chapel. Beyond is the Eastern Crypt which was built by William the Englishman, the architect who took over the work on the Trinity Chapel when William of Sens, the original designer, fell from the scaffolding and was killed.

Leave the crypt on the south side, cross the transept and turn right up the steps.

The Choir Screen and Bell Harry Tower

Half way up the steps in front of the Choir Screen looking up you will see the splendid fan vaulted ceiling of the Bell Harry Tower. It is both awe inspiringly beautiful and a magnificent feat of medieval engineering.

The Choir Screen (5) of the Six Kings was commissioned by Prior Chillenden in 1405 in keeping with the practice of separating the Choir from the Nave. Celebration of the Mass was hidden from public view by the choir screen and conducted in Latin until the Reformation when Henry VIII changed the national religion from Roman Catholic to Anglican. The statues left to right are: Henry V, Richard II, Ethelbert (first Christian King of Kent), St Edward the Confessor, Henry IV and Henry VI.

Pass through the screen in to the Choir.

Exquisite fan vaulting of the Bell Harry Tower, completed at the beginning of the 16th century.

The Choir

The Trinity Chapel and St Augustine's Chair.

Work on the present Choir began after a devastating fire in September 1174. It was based on the ruins of the burnt out structure but was extended east to include space for a shrine to St Thomas. It was designed by a Frenchman, William of Sens who introduced the newly evolving Gothic style to England.

The local building stone was flint so the cladding stone had to be imported from Caen in France. This light yellow stone was contrasted with columns of Purbeck Marble from Dorset and was the first use of polychrome stonework in England.

Thomas Becket's shrine was set directly behind the main altar in what is called the Trinity Chapel though architecturally it is an integral part of the choir.

The shrine became one of the most important places of pilgrimage in Christendom. The shrine was magnificent, its destruction by Henry VIII produced 3 cwt. of gold, 3 cwt. of silver and many precious stones, including one ruby as big as a man's thumbnail.

Stained Glass in the Choir

The North choir aisle contains some of the best stained glass in Europe. The glass not only illustrates Bible stories and historical events, it is a work of art in its own right. Whether it is medieval or modern, the glass is dynamic - full of life and colour. In our tour we can illustrate only two of these magnificent windows, the **Bible Windows (6)&(7)**. These famous windows are constructed from a series of circles and squares containing representations of Old and New Testament stories. The medieval scholars who chose the stories were illustrating the deep underlying harmony of the Old and New Testaments.

"The Old Testament is nothing but the New covered with a veil, and the New is nothing but the Old unveiled,"

City of God, St Augustine of Hippo.

This practice of juxtaposing stories, and the beliefs expressed by St Augustine, continued until the Council of Trent in 1545-63. The **Miracle Windows (8)** in the Trinity Chapel show the miraculous events which occurred at St Thomas's tomb.

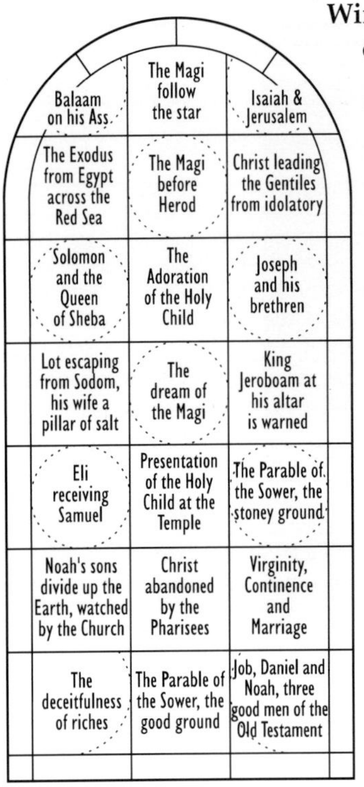

Bible Window (6)

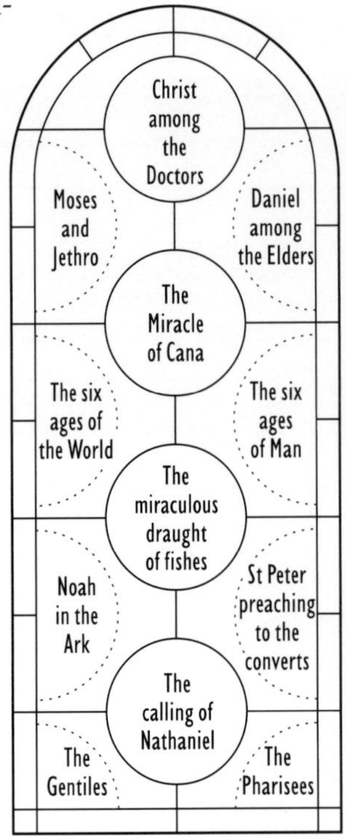

Bible Window (7)

The Sacred Pavement

In front of the **site of the shrine (9)** is a superb mosaic, the **Opus Alexandrinum (10)**. Designed in coloured stone its interlacing circles and squares illustrate the nature of the relationship between Man, represented by the earthly square, and God depicted by the eternal circle.

Notice also the large **round stone tiles (11)** depicting the virtues and vices, astrological symbols and the labours of the months. This zodiacal pavement was laid at about the same time as the Opus Alexandrinum to celebrate the moving of St Thomas's remains to the Choir in 1220. Once again the themes used show the natural, supernatural, moral and philosophical elements that were the keys of Medieval thought.

The stone chair or **Kathedra (12)** is called St Augustine's chair and has been used for the enthronement of Archbishops since the 13th century.

The Royal Burials

Canterbury has two royal tombs, Henry IV and his wife Joan of Navarre; and Edward the Black Prince. They command the prime positions either side of Becket's shrine.

On the north side of the Trinity Chapel is the **tomb of Henry IV (13)**. Most medieval kings were buried in Westminster Abbey and although Henry IV died whilst praying there he chose to be buried at Canterbury. Henry spent most of his youth fighting. He joined the Teutonic knights and visited Jerusalem before seizing the crown from Richard II at Flint

Key to the Roundels of the Sacred Pavement

The Labours of the Months

Jan - Janus, looks back to the old and forward to the New Year.
Feb - Man warming hands by a fire.
Mar - Digging.
April - Pruning a tree.
May - Man with a hawk.
June - Scything grass for hay.
July - Weeding with two tools.
Aug - Binding or reaping.
Sept - Riding, hunting.
Oct - Treading grapes.
Nov - Beating down acorns, for pigs?
Dec - Killing a pig?

Astrological Symbols

♒ - Aquarius, water carrier.
♓ - Pisces, two fish.
♈ - Aries, a ram.
♉ - Taurus, a bull.
♊ - Gemini, twins.
♋ - Cancer, 12 legged crab with the body of a scarab.
♌ - Leo, a lion.
♍ - Virgo, woman holding emblems of virtue.
♎ - Libra, woman with scales.
♏ - Scorpio, a genet (mongoose family)? or salamander?
♐ - Sagittarius, a centaur & bow.
♑ - Capricorn, a fish tailed goat.

Virtues Contending with Vices

Personified as women fighting monsters.
V1 - Self-control / Self-indulgence
V2 - Patience / Anger
V3 - Love / Envy
V4 - Humility / Arrogance
V5 - Diligence / Laziness
- Restraint / Gluttony
- Generosity / Greed

Beasts and Others

a - Leafy cross
b - Winged dragon with sword
c - Lion fighting a monster
d - Rabbit or hare playing a harp
e - Griffin

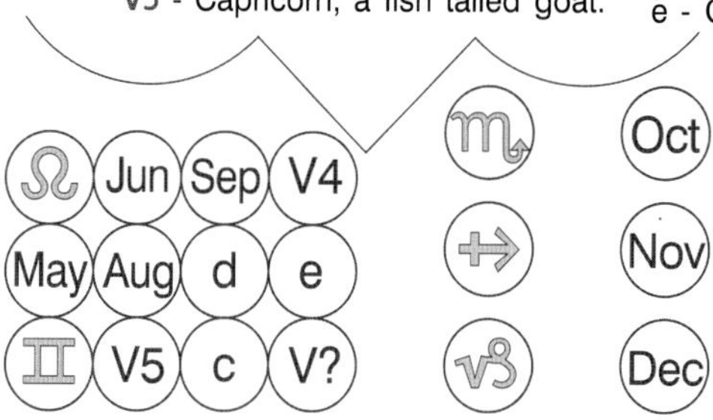

April, Cancer, Patience & Anger; and Griffin. Drawings by Julie Beer.

in 1399. He died in 1413 his body badly disfigured by leprosy. His life was immortalised by William Shakespeare in his play of that name. Henry's unpopular second wife, Joan of Navarre, died in 1437. They are portrayed in splendid alabaster carvings, under a canopy painted with their royal arms.

At the far end is the circular **Corona Chapel** today called the Chapel of Modern Martyrs. It was originally used to display another relic of St Thomas, a piece of his skull set in precious metals and gems.

On the south side of the Trinity Chapel lies the **tomb of Edward the Black Prince (14).** Edward, Prince of Wales, was born at Woodstock in 1330 son of Edward III. He inherited his father's military prowess. At the age of only 26 he was the victor at the Battle of Poitiers against overwhelming odds. It was during his Spanish campaign that he contracted an illness which was to mar the rest of his life and ultimately rob him of the Crown

To Whitstable & The University
0
1/8 mile
1/4 mile
0
1/4 km
1/2
To The
Canterbury West
LONDON ROAD
16
St Dunstan's Church
15
ST DUNSTAN'S STREET
ROPER ROAD
STATION ROAD WEST
ORCHARD STREET
14
P
THE CAUSEWAY
NORTH LANE
POUND LANE
Old Wool Store
LINDEN GROVE
WESTGATE GROVE
Westgate Museum
13
Westgate Hall
ST PETER'S LANE
Solly's Orchard
To London
The Guildhall (Holy Cross Ch)
Mayor's Parlour
12
Chaucer Heritage Centre
Blackfriars remains of Friary
WHITEHALL BRIDGE RD
WHITEHALL ROAD
WHITEHALL CL
Westgate Gardens
ST PETER'S STREET
TOWER WAY
St Peter's
Marlowe Theatre
Friends Meeting House
RHEIMS WAY
ST PETER'S PLACE
BLACK GRIFFIN LANE
THE FRIARS
Canterbu St Alph (Urban
Methodist Ch
11
ALL SAINTS LA
ST PETER'S GROVE
10
KING'S BRIDGE
Eastbridge Hospital
9
BEST LANE
Main Post Office
Royal M Art Gallery
8
Greyfriars Garden
HIGH STREET
43
Greyfriars remains of Friary
WHITE HORSE LA
GUILDHA STREE
Toddlers Cove
JEWRY LANE
7
Whitehall Medows
Canterbury Heritage Museum Poor Priests' Hospital
42
Great Stour Brewery & Museum
HAWKS LANE
Canterbury Tales
32
33
Visitor Information Centre
RHEIMS WAY
STOUR STREET
BEER CART LA
ST MARGARET'S ST
Marlowe Arcade
HOSPITAL LA
41
36
34
ROSE LA
PARK & RIDE pick up
CHURCH LA
ROSEMARY LA
ST JOHN'S LANE
35
GRAVEL
40
CASTLE STREET
37
ST MARYS ST
WATLING STREET
CASTLE ROW
MARLOWE AVENUE
Norman Castle Keep
GAS STREET
39
38
WORTHGATE PLACE
Dane John Gardens
Dane John Mound
City Wall Walk
PIN HILL
RHODAUS TOWN
WINCHEAP
GORDON ROAD
STATION ROAD EAST
Canterbury East
Police
To Ashford

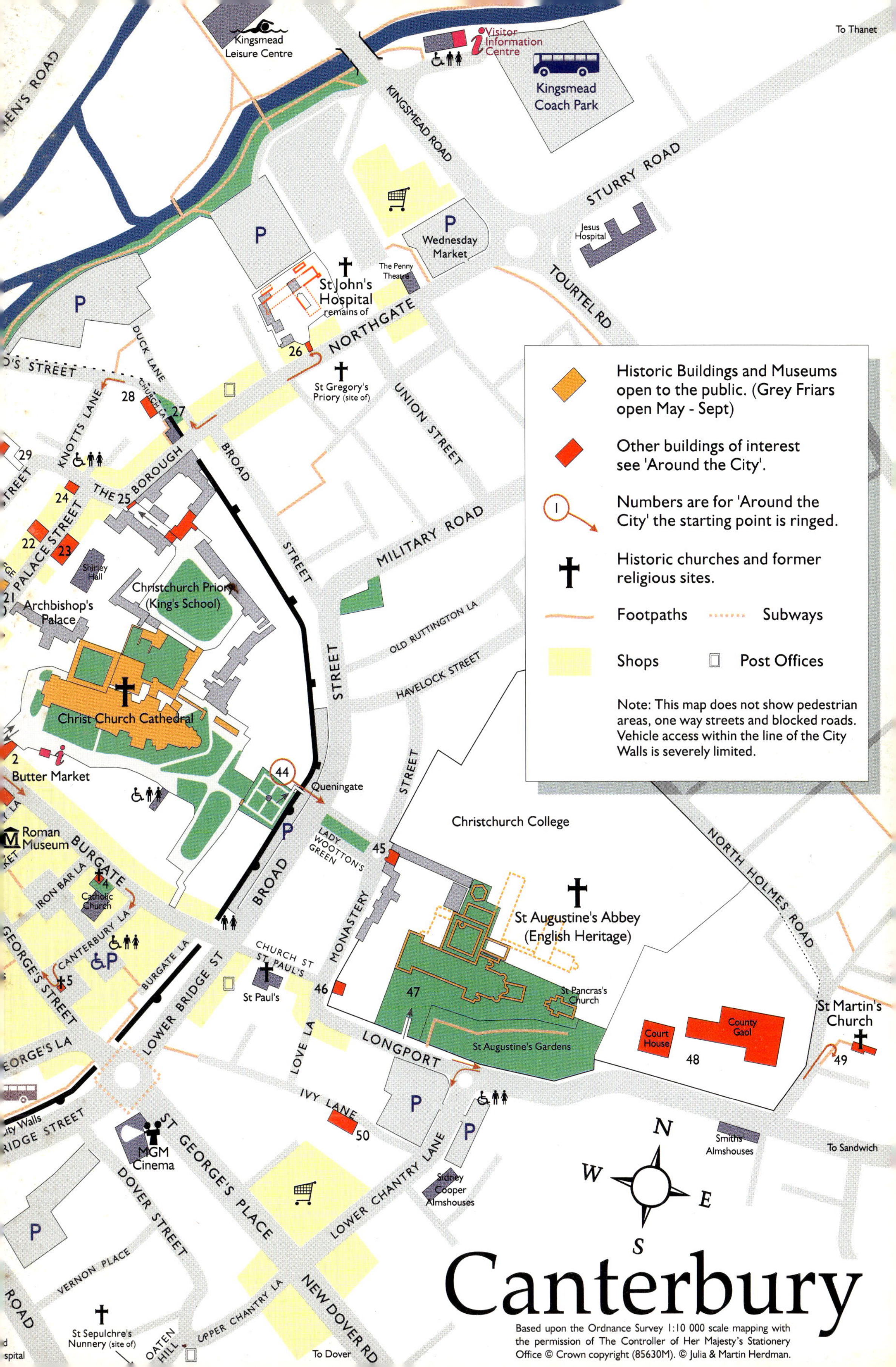

Kingsmead Leisure Centre
Visitor Information Centre
To Thanet
Kingsmead Coach Park
KINGSMEAD ROAD
STURRY ROAD
Jesus Hospital
Wednesday Market
The Penny Theatre
TOURTEL RD
St John's Hospital remains of
NORTHGATE
26
St Gregory's Priory (site of)
UNION STREET
DUCK LANE
CHURCH LA
28
27
KNOTTS LANE
29
BROAD STREET
THE BOROUGH
25
24
22
23
PALACE STREET
Shirley Hall
Christchurch Priory (King's School)
21
Archbishop's Palace
MILITARY ROAD
OLD RUTTINGTON LA
HAVELOCK STREET
Christ Church Cathedral
2
Butter Market
44
Queningate
Roman Museum
BURGATE
IRON BAR LA
4
Catholic Church
CANTERBURY LA
5
GEORGE'S STREET
BURGATE LA
LOWER BRIDGE ST
LADY WOOTTON'S GREEN
45
MONASTERY STREET
Christchurch College
NORTH HOLMES ROAD
St Augustine's Abbey (English Heritage)
CHURCH ST ST PAUL'S
St Paul's
46
47
St Pancras's Church
St Martin's Church
Court House
County Gaol
48
49
St Augustine's Gardens
LONGPORT
LOVE LA
IVY LANE
50
Smiths' Almshouses
To Sandwich
ST GEORGE'S PLACE
MGM Cinema
DOVER STREET
LOWER CHANTRY LANE
Sidney Cooper Almshouses
VERNON PLACE
UPPER CHANTRY LA
NEW DOVER RD
To Dover
OATEN HILL
St Sepulchre's Nunnery (site of)
N
W
E
S
Historic Buildings and Museums open to the public. (Grey Friars open May - Sept)
Other buildings of interest see 'Around the City'.
Numbers are for 'Around the City' the starting point is ringed.
Historic churches and former religious sites.
Footpaths
Subways
Shops
Post Offices
Note: This map does not show pedestrian areas, one way streets and blocked roads. Vehicle access within the line of the City Walls is severely limited.

Canterbury

of England. He died in 1376 shortly before the end of the 'Good Parliament'. Consequently he did not live to see the removal of the malign influence of his brother, John of Gaunt, and his father's mistress from the court. Educated at Canterbury, he asked to be buried in the Cathedral close to the chapel of Our Lady of the Undercroft in the crypt which he endowed, but the monks found it more fitting to place the tomb of such a great hero close to that of Becket. The elaborate tomb was constructed according to his will by his wife, Joan, who is more popularly known as 'the Fair Maid of Kent'. Replicas of his famous black armour are also on display.

Now continue around the south side of the choir and down the steps. End your tour of the Cathedral in the South West Transept where you will find the Warrior Chapel and the Gift Shop.

The Warrior Chapel, or St Michael's Chapel (15) houses the splendid funerary monument of Margaret Holland (d. 1439) and her two husbands, the Earl of Somerset and the Duke of Clarence. The wall monument to Thomas Thornhurst and his wife shows their three children each symbolically holding their mortality in their hands. The chapel also holds the flags, standards and battle honours of the Kent Regiments. There is a gallery dedicated to the history of the Kent Regiments at the Royal Museum in the High Street.

Tomb of Edward the Black Prince (14).

Around the Cit

This section of the book contains 5 guided walks, all starting from, or close to, the Cathedral. The numbers correspond to those on the centrefold map. Each walk starts with a red ringed number and arrow.

Many of Canterbury's most interesting and historic buildings are privately owned. Some can be visited while others may only be viewed from the outside. If you haven't eaten or you'd like to find an interesting cafe en route, look at the section 'Eating in Historic Settings' as many places of interest are now cafes and restaurants.

Walk 1 - The Centre &

Start this walk outside Christ Church Gate beginning with number 1 on the centrefold map.

The Butter Market - Burgate - Canterbury Lane - St Georges Street - High Street - King's Bridge

The Butter Market and Burgate

1 The Butter Market: This small market square was called the Bullstake, it now contains the city's main war memorial. This square and the streets in the immediate vicinity of the Cathedral contain some of the city's finest medieval buildings. Behind their claddings of mathematical tiles are many late medieval timbered buildings.

2 Cathedral Gate Hotel and Pizzaland: This charming building was originally constructed in 1437 as a medieval pilgrim hostel known as the Sun Inn. Although little of the 15th century building can be seen today part of the original west wall is exposed

Corner of the Butter Market & Burgate, formerly the Bull Inn (3).

Pilgrim Inns

in the restaurant.

3 Laura Ashley to Liberty: This handsomely restored building was once a 15th century pilgrim hostel called the Bull Inn. If you look up you will see that the building extends along Burgate from the Butter Market (formerly the Bullstake) but is now divided into shops. This exceptionally fine double-jettied timber-framed building was built by Prior Goldstone of Christ Church Priory between 1449-68 and much of the original building and roof remain. Parts of the cellar date back to around 1200.

> ## Mathematical Tiles
>
> 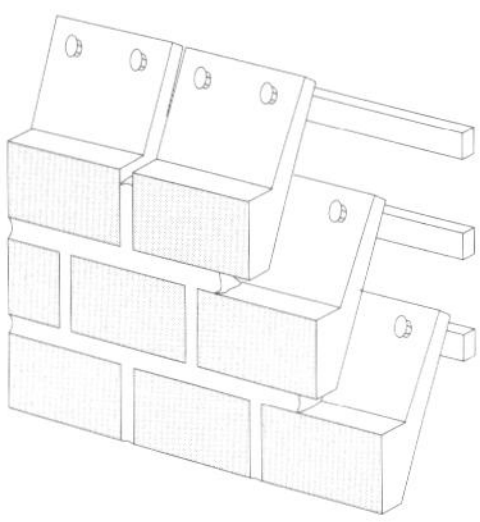
>
> Many of the buildings around the Butter Market are clad in this manner to make them look as though constructed of brick which was considered more fashionable in the early 19th century.

4 St Mary Magdalene Tower: This is the only remaining part of the medieval church of St Mary Magdalene which fell into disuse in the centuries following the Reformation. It now contains a rather beautiful sixteenth century monument. Exterior view only.

St George's Street

The St George's Street and Parade area were fire bombed in 1942 leaving only the tower of St George's Church standing. The post-war reconstruction has been preceded by archaeological investigations which have revealed a large Roman Bath House under

17th century plaster frieze on the Queen Elizabeth Restaurant (7).

Woolworth's and a large Roman apsed building near the Clock Tower.

5 Clock Tower: The only remaining part of the church of St George the Martyr where Christopher Marlowe was christened. The church was destroyed in a massive air raid in June 1942.

High Street

6 Samuel's Jewellers: On the corner of Mercery Lane. The walls of the Checker of Hope are the most obvious remains of a great 14th century pilgrim hostel built by Prior Chillenden, much of the building was destroyed by fire in 1865. This inn, built towards the end of Chaucer's life, would have been the destination for many Canterbury pilgrims. 'Next', opposite Boots the Chemists, was also built as a medieval pilgrim hostel.

7 Queen Elizabeth Restaurant: This fabulous 15th century building carries a superb 17th century plaster frieze known as pargeting across the front of the building. The first floor wood panelled room has a decorated plaster ceiling and is said to have been used by Elizabeth I to entertain a suitor, the French Prince Duc d'Alencon when the restaurant was part of the Crown Inn (1454-1774).

8 Royal Museum and Art Gallery: This splendid late Victorian building constructed in the then popular pseudo-medieval style was donated to the city by an expatriot Australian whose name it bears. See page 44 for details.

King's Bridge

9 The Eastbridge or St Thomas' Hospital was founded in 1180 as accommodation for poor pilgrims. It has a splendid Norman crypt which served as a pilgrims' dormitory and a 12th century refectory hall decorated with a 13th century painting of Christ blessing. The Christ figure is contained within a mandorla and is surrounded by the symbols of the four evangelists. There is also a splendid 13th century chapel. During the reign of Elizabeth I it was converted into accommodation for the elderly. See page 43 for details.

10 The Weaver's Coffee Shop: This medieval building consists of two structures joined together, one probably a hall type

Part of the once great 14th century pilgrim hostel the Checker of Hope (6).

The Weaver's (10).

house the other a shop. The building was converted to a loom shop by refugee Flemish weavers during the religious persecutions of the 16th century. Its gabled, diamond leaded windows and lovely riverside setting are extremely attractive.

This trail can be continued as Walk 2.

Walk 2 - To the Westgate and St Dunstan's

Start this walk at the King's Bridge beginning with number 11 on the centrefold map.

King's Bridge - St Peter's Street - St Dunstan's Street

St Peter's Street

The road through the Westgate is the traditional route for pilgrims entering the city from London and the north. Both St Dunstan's Street and St Peter's Street would have thronged to the sound of travellers feet and voices in medieval times. Today, the roads are equally busy with the traffic of modern commerce beyond the Westgate.

After the Weaver's Coffee Shop, to the right you will see a picturesque street, All Saints Lane, with medieval buildings, there is also a local pottery and small art gallery.

Timber framed houses, All Saints Lane.

The House of Agnes (14).

11 Red Rouge Café, Cogan House: This building is said to date back to 1190 and is probably the oldest house in the city although it is well camouflaged by the modern shop fronts. This beautiful building has a handsome Tudor wood panelled room and lovely garden.

12 Sidney Cooper Centre: Formerly the Canterbury School of Art, founded by Thomas Sidney Cooper RA (1803 - 1902) whose portraits and sketches of cattle and sheep were greatly admired in his day. Many pieces of his work are on display at the Royal Museum and Art Gallery. The Centre was presented in 1882 as a gallery. The Centre now serves as a Saturday, antiques and bric-a-brac market. Illustration page 47.

13 Westgate Tower Museum: The Westgate is the most impressive part of the city's defences. It was built in 1380 by Archbishop Simon of Sudley during the reign of the young king Richard II, the Black Prince's son. The weight of the new fortification was no defence against the rebellious citizens in 1381, when the city was pillaged over Parliament's imposition of a Poll Tax in the Peasant's Revolt. See page 44 for museum details.

St Dunstan's Street

14 The House of Agnes: Charles Dickens who set part of his story David Copperfield in Canterbury used this lovely building as the fictional setting of Agnes Wickfield's house where young David lodged while attending Dr Strong's School. Mr Wickfield employed the infamous Uriah Heep as his clerk.

15 The Roper Gate: This Tudor gateway once formed the entrance to the property of the Roper family. Margaret Roper was the daughter of Sir Thomas More, Henry VIII's Chancellor who was executed for his refusal to support the Act of Succession and the King's divorce from Catherine of Aragon. His body was buried in the Tower of London. After his decapitated head had been exhibited on Tower Bridge Margaret took it for burial at her local church, St Dunstan's. Sir Thomas was canonised by the Roman Catholic Church in 1935.

16 St Dunstan's Church: This church is not usually open except for services. It is dedicated to the 10th century Archbishop of Canterbury and great Cluniac church reformer. In the crypt lies the decapitated head of the martyr St Thomas More.

The Roper Gate (15).

Walk 3 - Palace Street and St John's Hospital

Start this walk by turning right as you leave Christ Church Gate. The route begins at number 17 on the centrefold map.

Sun Street - Palace Street - the Borough - Northgate - St Radigund's - Knotts Lane - King Street

Sun Street

Sun Street was the site of the medieval Rush Market, rushes were used for flooring, roofing and dipped in tallow to make cheap lights.

17 Cousin's the Jewellers: This prestigious jewellers shop was once the Sun Hotel where Charles Dickens stayed when in Canterbury. Look up at the gable end of the building to see the fine medieval timber work and window. Essential repairs in the early 1990's led to the covering plasterwork being removed. This exposed a typical medieval Kentish design with later herringbone brick infill. Exterior view only.

Cousin's the Jewellers (17).

Now follow the bend in the road to the right into Palace Street.

Palace Street

Palace Street derives its name from the Archbishop's Palace which stands on the east side of the street. The medieval Palace with its outbuildings and courtyards extended the length of the street. Lanfranc, the first Norman Archbishop of Canterbury re-routed the road to allow the Archbishop's Palace to be extended.

During the early 17th century the area was home to some notable families who left England for the New World on the *Mayflower* (1620) and the *Fortune* a year later. The ancestors of President Franklin D. Roosevelt and Winston Churchill hail from these streets.

18 Beaus Creperie: Formerly the Mayflower Restaurant, this building is said to be the house where Robert Cushman, after years of negotiations with the English monarch James I and the Dutch Prince of Orange, finally signed the contract for the hire of the Mayflower. The first pilgrim ship to America sailed from Plymouth, Devon to Plymouth, Massachusetts with 102 pilgrims on board on 6th September, 1620. No trace of the original building can be seen in the modern restaurant.

19 No. 51, Palace Street: Birth place of Mary Tourtel, creator of Rupert Bear, exterior view only. There is a special Rupert Bear exhibition at the Canterbury Heritage Museum. See page 43.

20 St Alphege Church Priest's House: Private dwelling, exterior view only. The Tudor frontage of this picturesque house with its voluptuous grotesques conceals a much earlier building behind. This house is probably one of the oldest in Canterbury and parts of it may date back to Norman times.

21 The Canterbury Centre, formerly St Alphege Church: This classic twin aisled Kentish church was once the centre of Huguenot (16th century Protestant refugees from France and Belgium) worship in Can-

Painted carving, Priest's House (20).

terbury. It was also the family church of the Cushmans; Robert Cushman was responsible for the hire of the Mayflower, first pilgrim ship to America. Today it houses historical and contemporary exhibitions on Canterbury life by the Urban Studies Centre. See page 44.

22 Conquest House: Antiques Shop. The 11th century cellar of this building is said to be the place Becket's murderers met before their dreadful deed. Today, you can see a beautiful wood panelled room with inglenook fire place. The building was heavily restored this century when the upper storey was added. Its 17th century appearance disguises what is a mainly 14th century house.

23 Archbishop's Palace Gate: The unimpressive flint building marks the ancient entrance of the Archbishop's Palace. This Tudor gatehouse suffered heavy restoration earlier this century and many of its original features have been obscured. In medieval times it led directly into the large outer court, separate from the Priory, containing the Archbishop's personal stables, barn, bakehouse, kitchen etc. Exterior view only.

24 Sir John Boys House: The leaning house of Canterbury is now a shop but is said to have been the home of an eminent and wealthy lawyer. Sir John Boys founded *Jesus Hospital* and a school for poor boys, just outside the city, in 1599. The house is early 17th century and has many decorative features including finely carved dragon posts (corner posts) on the ground and first floors. The house is timber framed with panels infilled with plasterwork intended to look like stone. This type of decoration would have needed guttering to protect it from the rain, which is unusual for a house of this date.

Sign on Beaus Creperie (18).

Sign on Conquest House (22).

The Borough and Northgate

At the end of Palace Street you enter the Borough and Northgate. To your left, behind the shops of the Borough were three narrow streets called Staplegate. Until the 19th century this area of the town lay outside both the Cathedral's and the Council's control. The small houses were havens for the city's villains and prostitutes. Today, the Northgate area has a village atmosphere and a strong sense of community.

25 Mint Yard Gate to the Cathedral: On the right you will see a gateway into the Cathedral grounds and the King's School. This gate is a Victorian replacement for the medieval gate, the remains of which can be seen, blocked, further along the street. The Mint Yard Gate was the main gate to the Priory and was used by tradesmen and those receiving charity from the Almoner. The name originates from the ancient coin mint which was once located there. The original gate, rebuilt in 1545, was blocked in 1903 when the school built a new gymnasium. Exterior view only.

Demon on gable Palace Street.

Now walk along the narrow pavement of the Borough into Northgate past St Radigund's and St John's Lane, on the left you will see the black and white timbered gateway of St John's Hospital.

26 St John's Hospital: Founded shortly after the Norman Conquest, it has two rows of alms houses with a church. The foundation, for 30 elderly men and 30 women, is one of the earliest in England. Archbishop Lanfranc probably chose the dedication to St John the Baptist because the saint was thought to have an affinity with monks, having led an austere and celibate life in the desert. The ruins date from the original foundation and at the back is one of the original lavatories, dating to the 11th century. St John's Hospital is a retirement home for the clergy but public access to the gardens is allowed. Steps into the gardens, exterior view only.

Priest's House, painted timber work (20).

Gatehouse, St John's Hospital (26).

If you have time, while returning to the city centre, there are some lovely buildings to see in the streets off Palace Street.

St Radigund's

27 City Wall Garden: This small sunken garden has a small portion of the Roman city wall exposed which was preserved because the medieval church of St Mary Northgate was built against it. The church was originally contained within the Roman gate which stood just around the corner in Northgate. It was demolished along with the gate in a road widening scheme in 1830. Only the church tower remains, encased in red brick, above. It is possible to see the outline of the small Norman windows high up in the wall. Steps into the garden.

28 Radigund's Hall: Simple Simon's pub and restaurant is housed in a classic Wealden house, a type of medieval house found in the Kent and Sussex Weald. It is late 15th century and originally consisted of a large hall, open to the rafters, with a pitched tile hearth in the floor forming a central fireplace. People and animals would have shared the accommodation but there were sleeping apartments at either end of the building on the first floor. See page 42.

King Street

29 The Old Synagogue: This beautiful 19th century Egyptian style synagogue was built to serve the city's small Jewish community. It is now owned by the King's School and used as a recital room. Exterior view only.

Continue along King Street until you reach the crossroads with St Alphege Lane to the left and Blackfriars Street to the right.

30 Dominican Priory (Blackfriars Street): There are only two buildings remaining from this monastic complex. The Refectory has been converted into an art centre by the King's School and can be seen at the end of Blackfriar's Lane. The Dominicans, who were also known as 'The Preachers', came to Canterbury from Europe in 1221. Both the refectory and the Guest Hall can best be viewed from Solly's Orchard over the river. Exterior view only.

The Old Synagogue, King Street (29).

Walk 4 - To the Castle and the Dane John

Leave the Cathedral through Christ Church gate and walk along the narrow medieval street directly ahead called Mercery Lane. This route begins at number 31 on the centrefold map.

Mercery Lane - St Margaret's Street - Castle Street - Gas Street - Church Lane - Stour Street

Mercery Lane - St Margaret's Street

The Checker of Hope: On the corner with the High Street is a jewellers (number 6 on the map). The stonework of the shop front once belonged to one of the largest and most magnificent pilgrim inns in Canterbury called the Checker of Hope. It was built by Christ Church Priory in 1392 and was largely destroyed by fire in 1865.

31 Pilgrim Lodging: On the corner of High Street and St Margaret's Street, opposite the Checker of Hope, you will see another three storey timber building, 'Next', which was also owned and used as pilgrim lodgings by Christ Church Priory.

32 The Old Fish Market: This classical style fish market has only recently been restored to its full glory. The siting of the fish market, which was moved from Burgate in 1500 on the instruction of the Mayor, led to one of the city's famous disputes with the Priory. The Prior who had lost the rent of the fish market in Burgate retaliated by bringing his own fish from Whitstable, this led to civil commotion with one Cathedral employee reportedly being swiped around the head with his own halibut!

33 Canterbury Tales: Formerly St Margaret's Church, now a themed historical experience based on Chaucer's Canterbury Tales. See page 43 for details.

34 The Crossroads: This irregular junction marks the centre of the Roman theatre which was constructed around AD 220. The theatre was a place of entertainment for the next two centuries. The Jutish settlers who

The Old Fish Market, St Margaret's Street (32).

moved into the abandoned town from the 5th century onwards may have used the theatre as a market place. A small part of the theatre's curved foundations are exposed in the basement bar of Alberry's and Slatters Hotel restaurant. See page 42.

At the end of St Margaret's Street turn left into Watling Street, the Roman road to Dover.

35 No.16 Watling Street: This 17th century building is probably the first brick house in Canterbury. The carved stone work was purchased from the Crown Commissioners when St Augustine's Abbey was demolished. Exterior view only. Return along Watling Street and turn left into Castle Street at the crossroads.

Castle Street

This is one of the most attractive streets in Canterbury with its mixture of architectural styles, commercial and domestic properties.

The only surviving building of the Greyfriars (43).

In earlier centuries it would not have been so pleasant. The Black Ditch, originally part of the castle earthworks was used for hundreds of years for the disposal of sewage. Later in the 19th century the gas works smothered the area in foul air.

36 Lullingstone House, No.5: This refaced 17th century house was the lifetime home of William Somner (1606-1669). Educated at the Kings School he was one of Canterbury's earliest historians. Across the street under the new buildings of 78/79 lie the remains of a Roman temple complex excavated in the late 1970's.

37 Castle Gardens: These lovely gardens are on the site of the long gone St Mary De Castro church.

38 The Kent Sessions House, No 28: This house stands on the site of the official residence of the Chief Constable of Kent who was keeper of the Castle. The present house was built in 1730 and incorporates part of the city wall. Private house, exterior view only.

39 The Norman Castle: Built between 1070-1094 the surviving keep is one of the largest in the country. Captured by the French Dauphin in 1216 and by Wat Tyler during the Peasants Revolt in 1381, it was also surrendered to Parliament during the Civil War. Until the reign of Elizabeth I the castle was used as a prison. It was here that many of the town's un-recanting Protestants met their deaths during the reign of Elizabeth's half-sister, Bloody Mary. In the 18th century attempts were made to knock the castle down but luckily they did not succeed. This splendid piece of Norman workmanship was left uncared for until 1928 when the local authority stepped in to preserve it for posterity.

This trail now returns to the centre of town via Stour Street and the Canterbury Heritage Museum.

An alternative route

You can return to the centre via the Dane John Gardens and walk part of the city wall (see centrefold map). Landscaped into the gardens is the Dane John Mound, which probably started as a Romano British burial mound. It was then reused by the Normans to support the timber defences of their first motte and bailey castle.

Continue by retracing your steps a short way along Castle street, take the first turning to the left, Gas Street. At the end of the lane turn right past St Mildred's Church.

Church Lane

40 St Mildred's Church: The interior of this disused church contains rare Saxon stonework. Mildred was the daughter of King Merewald and Queen Ermenburga of Kent. She was educated at a convent near Paris and later lived and became abbess of the nunnery founded by her mother at Minster-in-Thanet.

The ruins of the Norman Castle (39).

She died c.700 AD after a long illness. Her tomb became a place of pilgrimage and her relics were eventually removed to St Augustine's Abbey. Exterior view only.

Church yard of the lost church of St Mary de Castro, Castle Street.

Stour Street

41 'Maynard's Spital', The Maynard and Cotton Hospital: This series of almshouses were originally founded in the 12th century but the buildings you can see today date back to 1708. The money for the foundation came from coin minting and a pewter works. These small houses are still in use as retirement homes and have recently been extended to include two new dwellings. Exterior view only.

42 The Poor Priest's Hospital - Canterbury Heritage Museum: The Poor Priests or Grey Friars were followers of St Francis of Assisi who came to Canterbury from Italy in 1224. They first lodged at the Poor Priest's Hospital but later acquired their own land next to the river to build a complex of monastic buildings. The present building dates from the late 14th century. See page 43 for museum details.

43 The Greyfriars: Just off Stour Street, this lovely late 13th century building spans the river on two pointed arches and is the only surviving part of the original Friary complex. Access is only possible mid May to Sept, Mon-Sat from 2 to 4 pm.

Walk 5 - To St Augustine's Abbey and St Martin's Church

The Fyndon Gate, Lady Wootton's Green (45).

The Roman Queningate

The remnants of the original Queningate can be found buried within the city wall slightly to the north of the present gate, near one of the city wall towers. It is possible to see the filled in archway of the Roman gateway used by Queen Bertha and her priest if you look carefully at the wall. This small Roman foot-gate was used every day by the townspeople and monks for nearly 1200 years.

This walk starts at the Queningate number 44 on the centrefold map.

From the Cathedral the Queningate has steep steps which are difficult for push-chairs and impossible for wheelchair users. To avoid the steps leave the Cathedral by Christ Church Gate and turn left into Burgate and left again in to Lower Bridge Street.

Queningate - Lady Wootton's Green - Monastery Street - Longport - North Holmes Road - Ivy Lane

This walk follows in the footsteps of Bertha, first Christian Queen of Kent. The site of King Ethelbert's Saxon palace is as yet unknown but it is thought to have been within the city walls possibly in or around the Cathedral precincts. Queen Bertha and her personal priest are said to have used an old Roman building which stood on the site of St Martin's Church for their daily worship until Ethelbert allowed St Augustine to restore the city's Roman churches and build his new monastery outside the town.

Queningate

44 Queningate: The present gate dates from mid 15th century, this replaced the original Roman gate that Queen Bertha and her priest had used to leave the city by for their daily worship.

Lady Wootton's Green - Monastery Street

45 Fyndon Gate: Presently part of the King's School. This medieval gate completed in 1309 was once the main entrance to St Augustine's Abbey. The school buildings behind, which are mainly 19th century, incorporate the ruins of the Abbot's residence and the royal palace built for Anne of Cleaves. Exterior view only.

46 The Cemetery Gate: At the other end of Monastery Street you will see another, less elaborate, gate which was the entrance to the monks cemetery. Exterior view only.

Now follow the road round to the left into Longport.

Longport

This wide street was an ancient market place owned by the Abbey. Follow Longport Street until you reach the modern entrance to the Abbey ruins.

47 St Augustines Abbey: This important historic site is now protected by English Heritage. Here are the ruins of the first Benedictine community in England founded by St Augustine on land donated by King Ethelbert of Kent in AD 598, it is also the burial place of the early Canterbury saints. This once great monastery later became a royal palace for Anne of Cleaves. At its zenith the Abbey held one of the best medieval libraries in Britain and was a school of manuscript illumination. It is thought that the Bayeaux Tapestry may have been made here. Sadly the Abbey was dismantled stone by stone in the centuries following the dissolution of the monasteries, much of the stone disappearing into new buildings in the city. Occasionally fragments of beautifully carved stone from the Abbey are found by archaeologists as they excavate old cellars and walls. Today, you can walk around the peaceful ruins of four Saxon churches and remains of the medieval monastery. See page 43 for details.

Continuing along Longport Street you will come to Canterbury's old court house and prison on the left hand side.

48 County Gaol and House of Correction: This prison was built in a neo-classical style in 1808. Notice the reference to the Roman facis, the axes tied round with bundles of sticks, in the railings showing collective strength and security. The social and political background to the building of this rather attractive prison is one of war and popular discontent. It was a period of high food prices and rural unemployment. It is worth remembering that there were over one hundred capital offences on the statue book when this building was completed which ranged from murder to petty theft and industrial sabotage. Convicted felons still 'enjoy' Her Majesty's hospitality here but the court house is no longer in use. Exterior view only.

Now continue along Longport Street and turn left into North Holmes Road, St Martin's churchyard gate is straight ahead of you.

Ruins of the Abbey Church, St Augustine's Abbey (47).

North aisle window, St Augustine's Abbey Church (47).

North Holmes Road

49 St Martin's Church: This small parish church is the oldest in England. It is unlikely that the present building was used by Queen Bertha and her confessor before the arrival of St Augustine but the use of Roman brick and tile in the construction together with its mention by the Venerable Bede in his Ecclesiastical History must give the present church a very early foundation. St Martin of Tours, patron saint of the vineyards, was a popular saint amongst the Franks and the dedication may well date back to the time of Queen Bertha. Inside you will see not only a building of outstanding natural beauty but also the intricately carved 12th century font.

Return to the roundabout on Longport, turn left, then take the first right after the car park into Ivy Lane.

50 Ivy Lane, The Hall: About a third of the way down Ivy Lane on the left hand side you will see The Hall, a splendidly preserved medieval Wealden type house. Private dwelling, exterior view only.

Continue along Ivy Lane and back to the town centre via the subway at the roundabout.

Blocked Saxon door, St Martin's Church, (49).

Eating

The Butter Market.

Eating in Historic Canterbury

Canterbury has a multitude of cafes and restaurants spanning a broad range of qualities and prices. Many of the city's historic buildings house cafes and restaurants today. Eating in historic settings is an ideal way to see the inside of some of the town's most beautiful buildings. This guide does not recommend any of the establishments below but gives a simple description and map location.

Cathedral Gate Pizzaland: Butter Market (2). Originally built in 1437 as a medieval pilgrim hostel known as the Sun Inn it is now a modern pizza restaurant below with hotel above, part of the original west wall is exposed. Ground floor, some steps.

Liberty: Burgate (3). The Canterbury branch of the famous London store, this handsomely restored building was once a 15th century pilgrim hostel called the Bull Inn. The Tea Room is on the 1st floor, it is very popular, there is no lift.

Queen Elizabeth Restaurant: High Street (7). Fabulous 15th century building carrying a superb 17th century plaster frieze. 1st floor, no lift.

The Weavers Coffee Shop: St Peters Street (10). This medieval building is one of the most attractive in the city. Its riverside setting and gabled windows make it very popular. Steps down from the street, ground floor, some internal steps.

Beaus Creperie: Palace Street (18). No trace of the original building can be seen in the modern restaurant but the house is reputed to be the place where the contract for the hire of the Mayflower, first pilgrim ship to America, was signed. Ground floor.

The Canterbury Centre: Off Palace Street (21). This classic twin aisled Kentish church has been beautifully converted to provide exhibition space and cafe. The cafe and building are staffed mainly by volunteers, good value, always interesting, disabled access only.

Simple Simon's: Church Lane (28). This is a typical medieval house. The restaurant is upstairs, the bar downstairs is frequented mainly by young people. Steps, no disabled access.

Alberry's Wine Bar: St Margaret's Street. A small part of the curved foundations of the Roman Theatre are exposed in the floor of the basement bar. Steps. Also basement restaurant of Slatters Hotel opposite.

The WaterShed: The Old Wool Store, Pound Lane. This cafe-bar and restaurant is housed in an early 19th century warehouse built on the line of the medieval city wall next to the river.

Eating with children

Canterbury has many fast food restaurants, but if you want something other than burgers here is a list of places where you won't feel out of place with young children. Canterbury parks do not have picnic tables but the Westgate and Dane John gardens are both pleasant picnic spots.

Bhs: Marlowe Arcade, Rose Lane. 1st floor, lift, baby changing facilities.

Ricemans: Whitefriars Shopping Centre. 2nd Floor, lift.

Pavilion Cafe: C&H Fabrics, St Georges Street. 1st floor, lift.

Nasons: High Street and St Margaret's St. Coffee shop, ground floor; restaurant 1st Floor; steps.

The Canterbury Centre: St Alphege Lane.

Morelli's Restaurant: Longmarket. 1st floor, access by public lift in Longmarket or steps. Has a covered, paved courtyard with tables.

Pubs with gardens

None of the pubs offer facilities for wheelchair users.

The Dolphin Inn: St Radigund's Street. This pub has a large garden containing play equipment and a pets corner. Serves food and welcomes families.

The Three Compasses: St Peters Street. This high street pub offers a beer garden. Families with children welcome.

The White Hart: Worthgate Place. This pub has a particularly lovely garden. Serves food and welcomes families.

The Miller's Arms: Mill Lane. This pub does not have a garden but is situated next to the old mill race and Solley's Orchard. Patrons are permitted to sit next to the mill race and food will be served there if ordered at the bar. This is a very popular pub and service can be slow.

The Three Tuns: Beer Cart Lane. This pub has a large light and airy conservatory area where food and drinks are served.

Places to eat with easier access

This is a list of the best facilities in terms of accessibility and lavatories, no assessment of table heights has been made.

Bhs: Marlowe Arcade, Rose Lane. 1st floor, lift, disabled access and WC, Two entrances with steps, two without.

Ricemans: Whitefriars Shopping Centre. Use the main entrance opposite bus station. 2nd floor, lift, disabled access and WC on the 3rd floor.

Pavilion Cafe: C&H Fabrics, St Georges Street. 1st floor, lift, disabled access and WC.

The Canterbury Centre: St Alphege Lane. Ground floor, disabled access, no suitable WC.

Morelli's Restaurant: Longmarket. 1st floor, access by public lift in Longmarket, disabled WC. Has partially covered paved courtyard with tables.

Things to See and Do

The Poor Priest's Hospital (42), Canterbury Heritage Museum.

Museums and places of interest

Numbers in brackets refer to the City Map on page 24:

Canterbury Heritage Museum: Stour Street (42) Award winning museum depicting Canterbury's history. Modest admission charges with concessions for children, students, senior citizens and UB40. Family tickets and passport tickets to other Canterbury City Council museums are available. No WC, no disabled access.

Canterbury Tales: St Margaret's Street (33) Historically themed experience illustrating Chaucer's characters and tales with sights, sounds and smells from the period. Well done, but it can be a bit spooky for young children. Also gift shop, Medieval wine merchant, market and mint. Disabled access. Sun-Fri 10am-5.30pm, Sat and peak season 9.30am-5.30pm. £4.50, concessions for children, students, senior citizens. Family tickets £14 (2 adults, 3 children). WC inside Nasons, no disabled WC.

The Roman Museum: Butchery Lane. Excellent museum housing a magnificent Roman pavement. Mon-Sat 10am-4pm, also Sunday from March. For charges and concessions see Canterbury Heritage Museum. Disabled access & WC, lift, pushchairs must be left at reception.

The Eastbridge or St Thomas' Hospital: King's bridge (9) Pilgrim Hostel founded in 1180 with Norman crypt, 12th century refectory hall decorated with a 13th century painting of Christ blessing. No disabled access, steps, free Mon-Sat 10am-5pm, Sun 11am.

St Augustine's Abbey: Longport (47) Ruins of the first Benedictine community in England founded by St Augustine on land donated by King Ethelbert of Kent in AD 598. The burial place of the early Canterbury saints, this once great monastery later became a royal palace for Anne of Cleaves. Today, you can walk around the peaceful ruins of four Saxon churches and remains

Neck of a late 13th century decorated Saintonge jug from Gascony, recovered during the Longmarket excavation by the Canterbury Archaeological Trust.

of the medieval monastery. English Heritage: April-Oct, 10am-6pm, Nov-Mar 10am-4pm. Modest admission charges, concessions available. Access for visitors in wheelchairs (some steps). Public WC in Lower Chantry Lane car park.

The Great Stour Brewery and Museum: 75 Stour Street. This unique attraction offers the opportunity to brew your own real ales using up-to-date brewing equipment. Tours of the brewing rooms are available (last tour 5.30 weekdays and 4pm at weekends). Also: small museum, beer garden and brewery shop. Plans to expand the museum and shop are on the drawing board at the time of writing, so watch out for developments at the Visitor Centre. Open 10am - 6pm Mon- Sun, modest admission charges, concessions available, disabled access to brewery but not museum.

The Canterbury Centre: St Alphege Lane, off Palace Street (21) Beautifully converted medieval church with cafe showing historical and contemporary exhibitions on Canterbury life, staffed and run mainly by volunteers. Wed-Sat 10.30 am-5pm, small admission charge. Disabled access.

The Royal Museum and Art Gallery: High Street (8) Canterbury's main library is downstairs. There are paintings by 19th century Canterbury artist, Sidney Cooper, militaria from the Buffs Regiment and a miscellany of historical and archaeological artifacts upstairs. The exhibition gallery shows fine historical and contemporary art exhibitions. Free, 9am-5.30pm Mon-Sat. Disabled access to ground floor at rear of building, stairs, no lift. public WC at rear of building.

Westgate Tower Museum: (13) Shows the tower's use as a prison and garrison. An excellent view of the city and St Dunstan's Street is afforded from the top of the tower. Modest admission charges, see Canterbury Heritage Museum for details. No WC, stairs, no lift, no disabled access.

Canterbury Herbfarm and Perfumery: Broad Oak Road. A chance to see how essences are distilled for perfume manufacture. Also shop and demonstrations of flower arranging and aromatherapy. Open Mon-Sun, free, disabled access, parking.

The Great Stour Brewery, Stour Street.

Activities

Boat Hire and Trips:

Canterbury River Navigation Company: Punt trips start May, from Westgate Grove.

River Tours: Guided historic tours start Easter. Greyfriars to Miller's Arms, from All Saints Lane.

Also: Boat hire and tours, from King Street.

Horse & Carriage Tours: Available peak season only. See Visitor Centre for details.

Canterbury Guild of Guides: Walking Tours of the city. Also: Specialist walking tours during peak season and Canterbury Festival. See Visitor Centre for details.

Galleries

The Royal Museum and Art Gallery: See previous page.

Herbert Read Gallery: Kent Inst. Art & Design, New Dover Road. Shows large installation works, sculpture and paintings from home and abroad. Free. Oct-Jul, Mon-Fri, 10am-5pm. Refreshments, parking, no disabled access.

Tabor Gallery: All Saints Lane. Small privately run gallery and local pottery. Free. Mon-Sat. Ground floor.

Gibbs Gallery: 53 Palace Street. Small privately run gallery showing 4 exhibitions a year, mainly ceramics. Free, Mon-Sat 10am-5.30pm. Ground floor, steps.

Gardens

Chilham Castle: Beautiful gardens with lake and magnificent views. Raptor centre, deer park, 17th century house (not open to public), tea rooms and rose garden. Open daily from mid April. Modest admission charges.

Mount Ephraim, Hernhill: Gardens with lake, house (not open to public). Tea rooms, wine from the estate on sale. Open daily mid April-Sept. Modest admission charges.

Goodnestone Park, Wingham: Large gardens, tea rooms, house (open by arrangement). Open daily except Tue & Sat, April-October. Modest admission charges.

Sport and Leisure

See Visitor Centre for details.

Leisure Centre, Kingsmead: Pool and children's pool, gym, courts etc.

County Cricket, Old Dover Road: Kent County Ground. Watch out for special events, Cricket Week etc.

Greyhound Racing, Kingsmead: Regular meeting at one of the South East's premiere tracks.

Fishing, Fordwich: Canterbury District Angling Association, coarse and trout fishing, day permits available.

Holy Cross Ch. & the Westgate Gardens.

Wildlife

Howletts Wild Animal Park, Bekesbourne: World's largest collection of breeding tigers and gorillas. Excellent fun for all the family. Cafe, picnic area, free parking. Open daily except Christmas Day. 10am - dusk.

Brambles Wildlife Park, Herne Common: 20 acres of natural woodland with goats, donkeys, wallabies etc. Good family fun, excellent for smaller children. Cafe, under 5's playground and adventure play area for older children. Open daily, Easter - November. Modest admission charges.

Druidstone Wildlife Park, Honey Hill: Exotic birds, and animals. Open daily 9am-4.15pm. Modest admission charges.

Wingham Bird Park: Large exotic bird collection, pet village, lake, tea room, exhibition, picnic space and play area. Open daily except Christmas. Modest admission charges.

Oyster Fishery, Whitstable: Commercial oyster hatchery. Open Tue-Thur 10am-4pm and half term holidays May-Oct. Fresh oysters always available.

Bird Watching: Church Wood, Rough Common Road. RSPB mixed woodland reserve with parking, picnic space etc. Stodmarsh NCC wetland reserve, parking.

Cinemas, theatres and night life

The Marlowe Theatre: The Friars. Regional Theatre with restaurant and bar showing touring productions, music, dance and light entertainment. Tickets available from box office and the Visitor Centre, St Margaret's Street.

Gulbenkian Theatre: University of Kent. Medium sized theatre with cafe and bar showing touring productions, music, dance and comedy. Tickets available from box office and the Visitor Centre, St Margaret's Street.

Penny Theatre: Northgate. This small lively theatre is housed in the city's oldest theatre. Live rock bands, late night bar. Visitor Centre for details.

MGM Cinema: St Georges Place. 2 Screens. Telephone booking available.

Cinema 3: University of Kent, Cornwallis lecture theatre. Art films twice weekly during term time. Details from the Visitor Centre, St Margarets Street.

Restaurants with Live Music: Cate's Brasserie: Church Street St Pauls; Tapas Bar: Palace Street; Pizza Express: Best Lane; Flap Jacques: Castle Street (times vary, ask at Visitor Centre for details).

Information

Travel

Arriving by car - access within the line of the City Walls is severely limited. A Park & Ride scheme operates to the north and south of the town on the main A 28. Park & Ride buses are frequent and drop off in the city centre. Town centre parking is available, it is expensive and fills up early, especially on Saturdays.

Disabled parking - available within the city walls at Canterbury Lane, approach via Lower Bridge Street and Burgate, and at Orange Street, approach via Northgate and Palace Street.

Arriving by train - Canterbury East Station is on the London to Dover main line. Canterbury West Station is a rural line from Ashford to Ramsgate. Ashford connects to London and the Channel Tunnel. There is a subway with steps to cross from one platform to another at both stations.

Arriving at the coach park - facilities here include, toilets, cafe and information centre. It takes about 10 minutes to walk to the Cathedral, use the sign posts and the centrefold map for directions.

Access

Canterbury is a historic city, many of the pavements outside the pedestrianised city centre are narrow and uneven. The pedestrianised area is extremely busy, even on week days, the hustle and bustle can be quite daunting for young children. There are few public spaces and little public seating.

Most of the city's public buildings are historic, access to them for wheelchair users, mums with pushchairs, and those who find steps difficult, is poor.

Mother & Baby

Mothercare: Marlowe Arcade. Feeding and changing only, no WC.

Debenhams: Butter Market. 2nd Floor. Children's Wear department. Ask an assistant for the lift or use the escalator.

BHS: Marlowe Arcade. Ist floor.

Canterbury Lane: Public Lavatories. Toilet and changing room only.

Orange Street: Public Lavatories. Toilets and changing room only.